AT THE AUTOPSY
OF VASLAV NIJINSKY

AT THE AUTOPSY
OF VASLAV NIJINSKY

BRIDGET LOWE

Carnegie Mellon University Press
Pittsburgh 2013

Acknowledgments

Grateful acknowledgment is made to the publications in which some of these poems first appeared, sometimes in different form:

American Poetry Review: "Whatever You Thought Your Body to Be," "How the Pilgrim was Transformed"
Beloit Poetry Journal: "Blue and Red Ink Picture by Nijinsky in the Asylum"
Best American Poetry 2011, edited by Kevin Young and David Lehman: "The Pilgrim Is Bridled and Bespectacled"
Boston Review: "The Wild Boy of Aveyron Stands Up During a Dinner Arranged by the Doctor"
The Collagist: "The Forgotten Actress as Isadora Duncan in Russia"
Denver Quarterly: "Poem of Exile: Her Plea: Immortality as It Was Promised Her"
Drunken Boat: "God Is a Mathematician and In My Dreams," "The Pilgrim on the Shore"
Ghost Town: "Heaven," "I Am a Receptionist Who Is Not Afraid of Death,"
Grist: The Journal for Writers: "Animal Facing Left: A Sketch of the Wild Boy of Aveyron," "Portrait of Young Suburban Male as the Wild Boy of Aveyron"
Gwarlingo: "In My Study of Hysteria"
Kawsmouth: "The Forgotten Actress as Contestant on Dancing with the Stars," "The Forgotten Actress Dressed as Catwoman Alone in Her Room"
The New Republic: "At the Autopsy of Vaslav Nijinsky"
nthposition: "Poem for Virginia as Joan of Arc," "Poem for Virginia in Ecstasy"
Parnassus: "Proof," "Antoine-Laurent Lavoisier and Wife, Posing with Scientific Instruments Just Before He Is Beheaded"
Ploughshares: "The Pilgrim Is Bridled and Bespectacled," "Anti-Pastoral," "The Pilgrim Looks at the World from Above"
Salt Hill: "The Nihilist Takes a Bow," "The Gods Rush In like Police"
Sixth Finch: "Pygmalion"
Third Coast: "First Key Moments in the Construction of the Master Narrative"

Library of Congress Control Number 2012938560
ISBN 978-0-88748-563-3
Printed and bound in the United States of America

10 9 8 7 6 5 4 3 2 1

Contents

III.

IV.

for V.A.C.D.

It can be easily understood that a creature of this kind could excite only a momentary curiosity. People ran in crowds, they saw him without observing him, they passed judgment on him without knowing him, and spoke no more about him.

—"First Developments of the Young Savage of Aveyron,"
Jean-Marc-Gaspard Itard

I am a man, not a beast. . . . I am not a bloodthirsty animal. I am man. I am man.

—The Diary of Vaslav Nijinsky

I.

Poem for Virginia as Joan of Arc

In the form of a voice that hated you
your counsel came.

You lowered yourself
to the bathroom floor to hear it.

The world went slow as a drip of something
sugared. You couldn't speak

clearly. You stumbled over birds.
The call of God is gradual.

Alone you stood and flickered in the kitchen,
alone you stood on stage.

The dog stepped around you,
the television throbbed

a bruise-colored comfort, beacon for your bed-boat.
In the basement your father's waders

hung on a hook and, even out of water,
held the shape of a man.

You held the hand of a windowpane
and what sights it showed you, things it demanded!

When the time came to confess
what you'd seen a doctor was called

to hear you out. You were doubted because
you did not play at recess with the other girls.

You did not put flowers in your hair
or call a man a god.

Antoine-Laurent Lavoisier and Wife,
Posing with Scientific Instruments
Just Before He Is Beheaded

Good riddance, waved the small
handkerchiefs of the Republic, as the rational
became muddled, a mix of colors

pouring from my husband's severed head.
Wigged and alive, the two of us
were more like twins, his slender leg

that of a schoolgirl's, blond
curls rolling down my back. My blue sash.
In our portrait such illumination,

all around us light striking glass
and copper as I lean upon
my husband's shoulder, his elbow propped

on the red velvet tablecloth, a beaker
upturned at his foot.
How to know what to look for?

The dream is here, I thought, in this
pillared room, a pheasant quill
in his right hand, about to make something real.

The body is like fire, he wrote, it consumes
and gives off heat. It seemed
so romantic, like a love letter, like the tomb

disappearing under a current, briefly.
Like the word he invented—*oxygen*
for the steam that escaped my mouth.

In My Study of Hysteria

The sofa is pleather. My gorgeous thighs
stick in the late summer heat.
Your cigar is papier-mâché, but you keep insisting
it's real; you even light it,
in order to prove your genuine concern
for my concern for truth.

In my study of hysteria, we are riding on a train.
It is autumn now. I am tired.
My hair has turned gray just playing this game.
Someone boards the train and, Hitchcockian,
insists she is me. By now
I am stupid. I believe her.

The Wild Boy of Aveyron Stands Up
During a Dinner Arranged by the Doctor

Instinct, treasured dangerous thing, survival-sharp
and folded in the breast pocket of a loaned wool suit,
held behind his back, kept like a card in the sleeve,
worn around the neck on a string,
forest-honed into a thin talon of rigid bone
for ripping the meat of words into smaller pieces.

But now a limb withered against his chest,
curled lamb asleep before Lent, attendant
but only decorative, just there in case he needed it
as he stood up from his chair, and the fine point of his tongue
searched the cavity of his mouth and bits of heavy,
fragrant meat fell out.

And then the mouth began to make sounds,
choked howls groping for a vowel or a consonant,
at which point the other diners, guests of the doctor,
promptly put napkins in front of their faces
like what they'd witnessed was not only sacred but contagious,
as if they too might forget their own names.

The Forgotten Actress as
Contestant on *Dancing with the Stars*

You were a liberty horse, parading around
the ring without a rider. You needed no one
to direct you, to tell you where to turn.

It was like having the voice of God in your ear,
whispering your name over and over again,
lovingly. You were the body

left after a beheading—a stopped gap of time
in which you did not need a mind.
It was sublime.

Then they lined you up before a panel
of judges, who commented on your hairdo
and your technique, both of which

they found lacking. Cruelty came
like a surreal joke. The audience cheered
for more. You liked it.

THE FORGOTTEN ACTRESS AS
ISADORA DUNCAN IN RUSSIA

The Russians loved you. And for that,
you loved them back. It was maternal in a way,
on both sides. A country needing love, a woman
with a hole as big as a country in her chest.
They asked you to dance and how you obliged them!
Each rib bowed in graciousness, each fingertip
stretched toward the ceiling of paper stars
cut by children to light your way across
the stage. When you finished, your black head
of hair falling all forward, falling out, your body long
and starved, they stood and wept in honor of you.
They decorated you with scarves.

PYGMALION

The girls you loved in your youth—

under your bed, a blue box
of bodies posed

like dogs, the soft
focus shot taken from behind

of a girl spreading herself
open, showing you

the gleaming baby
rodent, wrinkled pink

anemone, inviting you, her head
turned, her mouth

hanging open. I would have done it
for you—

make them come
alive, I mean, make them

move their hands, touch
you, draw you toward them

in embrace.

Animal Facing Left,
a Sketch of the Wild Boy of Aveyron

Suggesting in profile or portraiture or two eyes
slicing their way through the jungle of another's
face, the tender soles of the feet from the climb up.

Suggesting distances seen by the animal, felt,
direction of the cardinal sort, a sense of it, as in
left and right, up and down, north and south.

Suggesting a painting against Victorian wallpaper
that was posed for, and a monstrous head
of hair that has been combed off the low forehead.

Suggesting a hallway, a dim corridor, an evolutionary
tunnel that everyone huddles at one end of, cheering
for you to travel through and be transformed.

Suggesting an up-and-comer with a camera and bottle
of water, touring the belly of the snake, taking pictures
in case we forget the concept, the theory of pain.

Suggesting the animal has dignity, which is more than desire
suppressed—while no one guessed a message from grief
would come catcalling, or the living thing beneath his breast.

The Pilgrim Is Bridled and Bespectacled

World, I honor you.
After everything
we've been through
I honor you

and take you with me
up the mountainside
where we will live
in wonderment.

I take you to the desert
where we shrivel like worms
and become tongues
for other people to kiss with.

World, there are two baskets
on my back.
Fill them. Fill them with fruit
and more fruit.

Or fill them with whatever
is customary
but tell me it is fruit.
Call it something good.

World, some have satisfied their thirst.
But I am the crying-out animal
who can see in the dark.
Forgive me.

At the Autopsy of Vaslav Nijinsky

They sliced the soles of his feet
open, lengthwise then crosswise

to see if there was some trick,
an explanation

for the man who could fly,
the man who saw the godhead

with his naked eye.
They pinned the flaps of skin

open like wings
and searched inside the gristle

for a machine,
a motor and spring, the wheel

inside the bone, the reason
why.

He must have been playing
a trick on them

all this time,
the wool pulled tight

over the collective cyclopic eye,
flashbulb-bright—

he must have, he must
have lied.

But the foot was that
of a normal man

after all, after all that
and they sewed the foot together again.

II.

Portrait of Young Suburban Male as the Wild Boy of Aveyron

As a teenager he would touch girls in their sleep.
Their bodies gave off some kind of heat
he sought.

His hands were dumb instruments
as he put them underneath their acrylic nightgowns,
compasses and protractors, things

bought to start the seventh grade
but never used to measure anything.

He would feel the ridges of their ribs
as he dragged a fingernail lightly across the skin
then down to the new hair

which he took as proof that everyone
was an animal somewhere.

Then in the morning he would wake for school
and the moon would be gone.

STATE LINE

She could fashion a noose from a hair bow. In Missouri, where she lived before, a man once told her that kindness was for dogs, not girls. Then: roll over.

The state line became a dream for her parents. They were match-people, stiff and breakable.
They marched their dry flints onto an acre of green wilderness and wept: Kansas!

The girl went off to play by herself and discovered a tree-house on stilts. The quality of height at night in a fort conquered!
And eating a candy bar while staring at the moon.

SAINT JOHN IN THE WILDERNESS

I was no longer beholding
the lamb of god

or any other
on command.

Banderoles
were meaningless, hieroglyphs
small

silent jokes
between long-dead
gods.

Ancient tongues
lashed me
in my sleep.

I bled. I tossed

as if a horse
throwing off the sea
foam, miles from shore.

I could not eat, bend
at the knee
anymore. Saint John

in the wilderness
was so close, I could almost
touch his face.

Leitmotif

I was devoted, I sat at your feet.
I called a photograph of a telephone
twenty times a day, asking for you, for you, for you.

I wore your ring until my hand fell off.
I put my hand on ice, my body under glass.
I slept a hundred years like that.

People came from distant lands to admire me.
My hair was preserved, a single flame.
Where were you?

When I awoke, I met a statue with your face.
It was as if no time had passed at all.
I bowed. I began

a polite conversation about weather.

Vaslav Nijinsky in 1919

I ran away from home. I ran and ran down the hill on which the house stood.
Ran and ran. I did not stumble. An unseen force was pushing me forward.
      —The Diary of Vaslav Nijinsky

The soul, dressed in red and blue,
didn't show through his suit.

Hungry, he paled. A sign?
He looked a woman deep in the face

until she gave him a cookie
and then another one.

In the winter all of St. Moritz Bad
closed down, closed down.

The whole town.

He wanted to lie down on the floor
or on the couch that had no cushions

but God said go so he went,
truth a snow-filled balloon

inside of him, swelling
by the minute.

Water and feed not vital
but appreciated.

So he ate the cookies quickly
before the doctor came to take him home again.

Anti-Pastoral

Your green Arcadian hills do not interest me.
The bird-bright eyes of every bird cared for,
the way it is promised, the way it is written,
everyone fat on their share of sun and seed.

But I don't see you in the dark streak of a cat
crossing the street or the regal skunk in summer's heat
that strolls the sidewalk after dark, stopping to look at me
before moving on to its home under a neighbor's porch,
pushing its black-white weight through the latticework.

I don't see you in a head of lettuce, decapitated
and wet at the grocery store, singing in Orphic dissonance.
I look at your trees and see the night my mind rose up
and left the body's bed, the skin of the moon
in your teeth.

I begged you to make the mule of my mind
come back. Do you remember what you said?
Nothing. And in the silence after that—
my head without my body, singing on the riverbed.

The Forgotten Actress Heckles
an Important Man at an Awards Dinner in L.A.

You felt impatient. There were so many things
to eat there. And everyone kept raising their
drink. All hail someone or something! So you drank
until the room came into focus in a kind of
internal way. There were so many people there
in suits and dresses. What did they want?
You had not eaten in days. You knew that
most of what came out of a mouth and, conversely,
what went into a mouth, was bile. Most days
you tried to turn your mouth into a brick wall.
You focused on not moving your tongue
into crevices, dare it exercise the muscle or find
a morsel. It felt like purification, it felt so sure.
Then you opened your mouth like a door and stepped
through into the fire (how it poured!) until
you were carried out of the ballroom by your elbows.

First Key Moments in the Construction of the Master Narrative

Doing the doggy paddle to keep up.

Mistaking prerecorded operator voices for human beings.

Asking the voices over to your house.

Waiting on your front stoop with a plate of deviled eggs.

Loaning the voices money when they call again.

Handing over your first born gerbil.

Bobbing for an apple at a Halloween party.

Practically drowning.

Something repeatedly getting in the way of the apple.

Hair from your wig or a string from your cape.

You hold up the line and everyone hates you.

Someone asks, What are you anyway?

And you lie. You make something up.

The Gods Rush In like Police

In their vinyl hats and gloves, patent leather
reflector vests, glitter falling from the sky.
In unison, the hairy knuckles of their hands
work to grip the melted door and free you.
The gods wear polyester shorts and tennis
shoes, sport mustaches trimmed
with unearthly precision. The gods like cock
and they are proud of it. They dance
and everything is episodic in the worst way, a rerun
of a rerun of *Three's Company*—a scenario
you've seen before, certain of the outcome
but tempted to watch it all play out. *Macho, Macho Man,*
the gods are chanting, and you believe them,
you believe them! The gods draw you
a chalk line, they force you to walk it
like a plank down the side street of your childhood.

The Pilgrim Looks at the World from Above

I want this life, full of dogs and people.
The trick is not stopping.
The dead sleep like bugs tucked into matchboxes

while the living imitate life
within the confines of pink and green lines,
denoting states.

And I see you wandering the labyrinth
of your dumb animal existence,
your body warm, seeking exit.

Somewhere a man takes out his teeth.
The body is a series of reductions, losses.

Parasitic longing worms its way into his back.
He rolls onto his other side
and turns off the light, seeking comfort.

Seeking comfort you have done everything
but die.

I see you turning corners and pulling at your hair.
I see you weeping against the wall
that is always there.

And in daydreams I dare to see you
delivered into an open field,
a vast space on the map where a creek flows

and nothing can stop it, the feeling,
the love you have for your life,
for your very own animal body

which has delivered you there
in time, just in time.

III.

The Nihilist Takes a Bow

A rigged coin toss concludes.
Nero plays a happy tune
on his portable radio.
He keeps winking at me
from his wicker wheelchair, pointing to his lap.
Someone takes my photograph
from behind a potted plant
and puts it on the Internet. Is this my fantasy?
It's so small and cross-eyed.
I press my face into the Astroturf.
The stage is strewn with my body.
From miles away I can still see
you—crowned and bloated, consulting a mirror
on the status of the future
of your hairline.

THE DOCTOR, DRUNK, GIVES THE WILD BOY OF AVEYRON ADVICE ON WOMEN AND SEX

Aspire to love less and ever less.
Don't try too hard to please them or undress
them. They often tend to congregate
near water, swans that hover over their own
beauty. Their flesh is something sensitive
to sting, but they seem to have a fetish
for the pain. Sting a young one and she'll bleed.
Oh go on, lie across your bed and weep!
Regret the day you ever raised a comb!
Or seek the thing that pricks you with its heat,
use the tricks you learned while on your own
and remember, look for beauty—men don't quench
the body's thirst in any dog-eared slit.
At least be sure her name is somewhat known.

SAINT JOHN IN THE WILDERNESS, II

He was the playmate
of the gentle one

whose tears fell
upon my lips.

Who told me the secret
of love—

your body
will be shit on, and I alone

will understand.

Underwater, in the bathtub,
looking up,

I could see him
in stains

upon the ceiling—
his hair thick

and fawn-colored,
his eyes

small arms, his mouth
a cradle.

Whatever You Thought Your Body to Be

Whatever you thought your body to be,
vessel for hubris, trapdoor to the soul,
sight for sore eyes or heavenly vision,
rack of flesh with nothing to offer at all.
A temple of the holy ghost, a ghost,
black hole for dogs to bury their bones.
The dog in heat who offers herself,
the offering itself or the heat alone.
Place for men to lay their heads and die,
plank of wood that leads to the sea.
Whatever you thought your body to be,
see it out walking, forgetting your name
and the presents you gave it for all its birthdays
and the ways that you loved it and didn't.

GOD IS A MATHEMATICIAN AND IN MY DREAMS

God is a mathematician and in my dreams
I'm held down while my head is wrapped in netting
and strangers lick between my legs and laugh.
Then my legs are bent into various triangular shapes
and their degrees measured and recorded with tiny pencils
and photographed for an award-winning textbook.
Only a mathematician would let that happen.
Only a mathematician would force me
to the front of the room when I didn't know
the answer to a problem, thereby requiring me to draw
a picture of the male anatomy, bulbous and hairy,
in order to maintain my pride, control, and honor. I rode
your 8ᵗʰ grade chalkboard like a fucking horse, my horse,
my stallion, and even today, Mr. Company, I reject
the equation you have left like a week old dinner
for me to eat and eat at your wicked and loveless table.

Proof

It is said that Catherine the Great
requested the mathematician Euler
confront Diderot, atheist, with this:

"Sir, $(a+bn)/n=x$,
hence God exists. Reply!"

There was a long silence as Catherine
crossed her legs and Diderot turned
and fled like a barn cat from fire, an "x"

solved for as useless, eliminated.
But Pythagoras—who heard the cry
of his dead friend in the bark of a dog

and could flash a golden thigh
like some barroom harlot, who rejoiced
in the perfect spirals of seashells

and pinecones, who had lived four lives
that he remembered in detail and believed
that the mind was the key to the heart—

laughed at the folly of this display
from his perch in the castle rafters
where he was currently living his fifth life as a bird.

Heaven

The villagers are reading hot guts
and drinking tonics. I'm relaxing
on a rock, sunning my midsection,
my delicate white legs.
The palm trees stand stiff
in the wind, archaic, shyly optimistic,
foreign. A Cuban boy
presents me with a muffin, his homeland
a mere neck's-turn away.
My hair blows this way
and that, as if I'm the featured guest
in a music video from my childhood.
For every broken heart, one golf course.
Everything comes out even.
The birds call me by name, and while
I'm distracted, fish heap themselves
into my basket. And the loaves,
the loaves! They multiply.

Eat Not the Heart, Neither the Brain

Or eat the heart but salt it.
Roll it in spices because how very bland
it has become in the unending filth of your hands.
But save the brain.

Or eat that too but know that it will be cool
and heavy on your tongue
and capable of great calculation.
It calculates your beastliness as you eat.

Eat them both undercooked, without silverware.
Or sauté them in butter and garlic,
coaxing their bodies, snail-like, from my
carcass. Slide them like oysters

into the dank cave of your mouth.
Light candles, wear a suit.
Put a roof over their heads, promise
each the biggest bedroom.

But listen to me when I tell you
the soul is something best avoided.
Or don't. Who am I
to warn of what you'll suffer.

Achilles and Penthesilea

Once, he stumbled on a fallen body—
an Amazonian queen, her bow bereft, her mouth dry
and open to the wind.

He recognized her scent, remembered
the way she carried herself around the camp, her proud
breast, the whiteness of her skin.

He found himself more turned on than ever, his tongue
thick as if bee-stung, eager to touch something
or someone. He stood over her and unzipped.

She was already forest-bound, her bow restrung,
in the company of the elegant hounds
of her childhood. He knelt before her

face, whispering: *mein Liebe, mein Leben, mein Kampf*
until the opalescent loam rushed forth,
covering her lips, filling her still-open eyes.

You Come Back to Me
as This Feeling from Childhood

I spelled my name over and over again
in snow.

I sat alone at the kitchen table, a long plank
of ruddy wood lit from above
by a brass dome.

I did my homework. The indifference of objects
hurt me. I wore a skirt
to school every day, and a cardigan.

Sometimes I preferred to lie
down flat, to think of nothing with my mouth
open, or stand stoic in the field

while flies lit on my eyes.

IV.

The Pilgrim on the Shore

Dear pink genital, you alone oblige me.
Meanwhile no one writes. This hand is tired,
I tell the sky. Where is the fleet, where
the horizon? I can hardly lift my head
to see the small, sand-colored shapes
waving from their buggies like maggots.
It's a picture from childhood,
that faraway, that sweet.
Dear old friend, all this time it was you
calling my name in strange places.
Dear physic, I'm sicker than you are strong.
Bring word to your brothers and sisters:
the villagers are hostile and inside me.
Somewhere in the distance there's fire.

Poem for Virginia in Ecstasy

Tell me.
Tell me all about it.

The curb you laid down in,
waiting for the ambulance
like it was your chariot.

Your cry
pinging off artificial trees,
the branches hollow reeds

you play as woodwinds,
classical tunes, untaught
in your brutal version of a forest

where the heart takes precedence,
center stage, and the set
is plywood and wallpaper

and everything clean,
entrances and exits controlled
by the deft hand of a director no one can see.

You fall in love with the director
no one can see
over and over again,

then call from the nest
you've built in a high tree,
catching clouds on your tongue

and throwing them up,
purging yourself of the pleasure
his arrogant hand has made.

In terms of transgressions,
no one has died—no,
not even Christ

who doesn't recognize you,
writhing there at his feet.
My friend, my love!

Even the worm that circles
the wet black orb
of the dead bird's eye

knows better than you.
It won't get what it wants.
Beggars never do.

Blue and Red Ink Picture
by Nijinsky in the Asylum

The crossed angry eyes,
the double tusks.

Not in a child's hand
because not a child's story,

though perhaps the exact darkness
a child at night

in a bedroom knows,
a child's mind alone—

the bedroom a broom closet,
the child's body the broom

and the straw of the broom like hair
cropped close to the skull.

Prayer

Bend me so my filth is most apparent.
Stretch me past the point where flesh still gives.
Give me all the things I never wanted.
Save me from this strange and loveless thing
I've become. Perfume me with the oil of the sorry.
Help me to be eager for the white-hot whip
of heaven, for the thunderbolt, for the reins
you hold in earnest do not hurt me.
I don't deserve the reins you hold in earnest.
Is it you who will keep steadfast by my side?
The arrows fly. Meanwhile the bird watches,
a thousand tricks in its black, million-sided eye.
I moan, I beat, I tear my garment in my
heat, in my love, O Lord, your name is like a bird
to me, your name is like a bird which imitates
but does not truly speak.

The Forgotten Actress
Dressed as Catwoman Alone in Her Room

There were so many nights of loneliness, the word
prowl comes to mind, the needle and thread
were as bored as I.

My mind was elsewhere.
The front stoop, crying. I operated solo.
I was living in New York at the time.

My closet was full of demure clothing
for positions like secretary and teacher, the demeaning
wardrobe of the demeaned.

A woman on her knees
understands what it's like when people look
and think they see you.

We all have a part to play, the nuns liked to say,
in the Lord's universe.
I knew that this was mine.

A Washerwoman's Account, Aveyron, 1799

At first it seemed a beast, backward
in its way of walking, with a wild beard over half its body
as its limbs moved wrongly through the trees.
I looked for wings or beak but found him standing
on two feet, more like a man than not.
Sunlight was coming through in places
so that his face was briefly shown to me—
a fruit fallen and then trod on,
raked by birds and vermin for the seeds.
When word spread of what I'd seen
I was asked to tell my story in a formal manner
before a team of doctors and officials,
for a written account to be published in some kind of paper.
Instead I told them it was an ordinary day
and that I had simply wanted some attention
from my husband, who lately has been
eyeing other women, and so
had dreamed the creature as a way to turn his head,
if only for a minute and out of pity.

Her Plea: Immortality as It Was Promised Her

_____, Master, Friend,
you're wrong. We don't go on

in words. I'm sick
of these black marks across the page.

They should be a ladder.
They should be Lethe and you should be

waiting for me on the other side
in all your fame and glory.

At least extend a rung.
But no, it's just chicken scratches

in the sand, a real
joke, this path just a short

length of rope, about from here
to that tree. Yes I see

possibility in the earthly
body, that sewer system we carry

atop our legs but I know I will not
branch or leaf, I know

my insides are wet pig flesh
shining. Is it proof

you wanted? I thought these things
were settled. I thought

these black shapes were boats
away from myself but they're stones

in every pocket, anchors
on each wrist.

I Am a Receptionist Who Is Not Afraid of Death

Your balls release their last mediocre fruits
across the torso of a corpse
who loves you. It feels so good,
being loved. It is your favorite feeling.
You want to feel it all the time.
Do white worms dance on the necrophiliac's grave?
you asked your mother when you were five.
Yes, white worms dance
on the necrophiliac's grave and the graves of all
who defile. You have a wolf's jaw
and stretch the muscles of your face back to prove it.
Inside the sheep's clothing is a sheep.
Somehow I've ended up
at the mall again, with a plastic bag
over my head, whispering the Lord's prayer
to every bench and fountain. Come back, I say
to the water disappearing down a hole. And it does—
it drips from the cherub's stony baby dick.

Folk Song from the Region of Aveyron

My mouth is a flute
other people whistle through
and afterward do not bother to clean.

Oh the world is cold and mean!

I feel the way my jaw juts,
knowing nothing.

And you better keep your armpits clean!

The whites of my eyes:
iridescent slime
worms leave under bricks.

Lord is a word I love to say.

In case He comes your wares to glean!

My asshole is a wound that weeps.
Dogs stand far off from me,
an alarming smell.

And your body to make a neat machine!

My forehead goes before me
always, brave little pilgrim of industry.

Oh Lord, tra-la, tra-la!

How the Pilgrim Was Transformed

Not by a vision, not by a task.
Not by a voice from above.
Not by crying out.

Not by a horse riding fast.
Not by death or desire.
Not by the desire for death.

Not by getting slit from belly to throat.
Not by stealing the breath of an infant child as it sleeps.
Not by telling a loved one a dream.

Maybe by a vision.
Maybe by the completion of a very difficult task.
But what is the vision? What is the task?

All I know is this:
I thought love would save me.
No—I really thought that.

By grief, always by great grief.

Notes

Epigraph from "First Developments of the Young Savage" is taken from *The Wild Boy of Aveyron (L'enfant sauvage)* by Jean-Marc-Gaspard Itard, translated by George and Muriel Humphrey.

The Nijinsky poems and poem titles are directly inspired by *The Diary of Vaslav Nijinsky* and its photographic captions. Epigraphs are taken from *The Diary of Vaslav Nijinksy*, edited by Romola Nijinsky, University of California Press.

Some titles for the Pilgrim poems have been taken or adapted from the 17th century Czech text *The Labyrinth of the World and the Paradise of the Heart* by Jan Amos Komenský.

"The Forgotten Actress" poems are for and about the American actress Sean Young.